Get On Board!

we hear our conductor
singing low
the song she uses
to let us know
now is the time
to get on board

the train we ride
won't run on a track
we're heading north
not coming back
we brave our fear
to get on board

the midnight train
runs underground
we hide and pray
not to be found
we risk our lives
to stay on board

station houses
along the way
take us toward
a brand-new day
we *will* live free
so get on board!

Summer days were mowing days in Colchester, Ontario. Elijah McCoy watched his father cut the tall grass. He was waiting for the machine to break. When it did, he jumped for joy. Elijah was only six, but already he was good at tinkering with tools.

ALL ABOARD!

ELIJAH MCCOY'S STEAM ENGINE

Monica Kulling   *Illustrated by Bill Slavin*

TUNDRA BOOKS

*For Nancy,
who dreams of riding the rails
from coast to coast*

M.K.

*For my father,
the inventor*

B.S.

Thank you to Kathy Lowinger and Sue Tate for welcoming me to Tundra Books. I appreciate your enthusiasm and professionalism. And guess what? I'm still pinching myself!

Andrew Moodie's beautiful play *The Real McCoy* inspired me to write this story.

Paperback edition published by Tundra Books, 2013

Text copyright © 2010 by Monica Kulling
Illustrations copyright © 2010 by Bill Slavin

Published in Canada by Tundra Books,
a division of Random House of Canada Limited,
One Toronto Street, Suite 300, Toronto, Ontario M5C 2V6

Published in the United States by Tundra Books of Northern New York,
P.O. Box 1030, Plattsburgh, New York 12901

Library of Congress Control Number: 2009937952

Library and Archives Canada Cataloguing in Publication

Kulling, Monica, 1952-
        All aboard! : Elijah McCoy's steam engine / Monica Kulling ; illustrated by Bill Slavin.

(Great idea series)
For ages 5-8.
ISBN 978-0-88776-945-0 (bound). – ISBN 978-1-77049-514-2 (pbk.)

        1. McCoy, Elijah, 1844-1929 – Juvenile literature. 2. African American inventors – Biography – Juvenile literature. 3. Lubrication systems – Juvenile literature. I. Slavin, Bill II. Title. III. Series: Great idea series

T40.M33K84 2010   j609.2   C2009-905772-7

We acknowledge the financial support of the Government of Canada through the Canada Book Fund and that of the Government of Ontario through the Ontario Media Development Corporation's Ontario Book Initiative. We further acknowledge the support of the Canada Council for the Arts and the Ontario Arts Council for our publishing program.

ONTARIO ARTS COUNCIL
CONSEIL DES ARTS DE L'ONTARIO

Edited by Sue Tate
Designed by Leah Springate
The artwork in this book was rendered in pen and ink with watercolor on paper.

www.tundrabooks.com

Printed and bound in China

2 3 4 5 6   18 17 16 15 14 13

Elijah McCoy was born in 1844. His parents had
come to Canada on the Underground Railroad. They
didn't talk much about the slave days. Elijah and his
eleven brothers and sisters kept them busy.

Elijah's mother and father saved every penny they
could to send Elijah to school. At sixteen, he crossed
the ocean to study in Scotland. Elijah had a dream: he
wanted to work with machines. He wanted to become a
mechanical engineer.

In 1866, Elijah finished school in Scotland. His family now lived in Michigan. One day, a locomotive rolled into the station with Elijah on board. His mind was crackling with ideas. In Michigan, he was going to be an engineer!

Elijah went looking for work at the Michigan Central Railroad.

"It takes learnin' to be an engineer," said the boss, spitting at Elijah's feet. "I got ashcat work if you wannit. Ain't hard. You bail it in. You grease the pig."

"Excuse me?" said Elijah.

"You shovel coal into the firebox," replied the boss, slowly. "You oil the wheels. You oil the bearings. It's not hard."

What a letdown! Elijah knew engines inside out. He knew how to design them. He knew how to build them. He also knew the boss didn't think much of him because he was Black. But Elijah needed work, so he took the job.

The steam locomotive was exciting. People called it the Iron Horse. It was a fire-breathing monster. When it had a head of steam, it was faster than a horse and buggy!

Feeding coal into the firebox was hot, hard work. It was also tricky. The fire boiled the water. The boiling water made steam. The steam worked the machinery. If the fire got too hot, the boiler might explode. If it wasn't hot enough, the train wouldn't move. Or it couldn't climb the smallest hill.

Elijah went to work in old clothes. An ashcat's job was a dirty one. Soon Elijah was covered in soot and cinders.

A boy was under the train. His clothes smelled of oil.

"That's your grease monkey," said the boss. "He'll oil the places you can't get to."

A grease monkey was paid pennies a day. At night he slept on the train's grimy floor. The work was dangerous, and boys often got hurt. Or worse.

There has to be a safer way, thought Elijah.

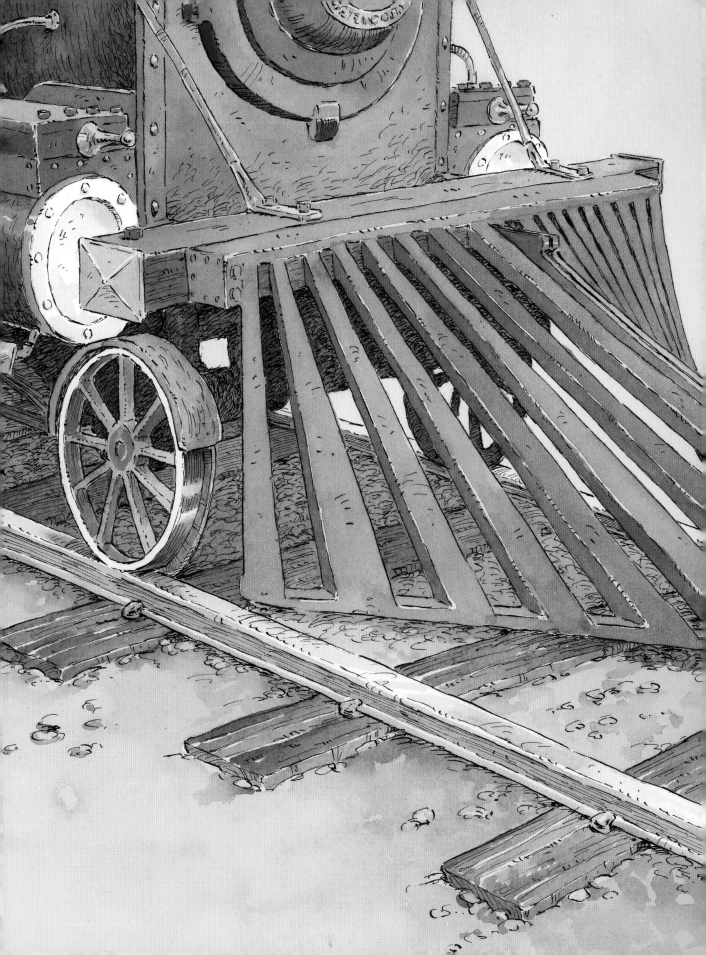

Elijah baled in the coal as fast as he could. Sweat poured down his face. His hands were raw. The water in the boiler took time to heat up. While Elijah baled, the grease monkey clambered around, oiling. Finally, the train was tanked up, ready for its run.

The engine huffed and puffed. Smoke billowed from its stack. The wheels clacked. The locomotive chugged along for about half an hour. *Chug! Chug! Chug!*

Suddenly, *screeeeech!* The train stopped cold. The boy hopped down and crawled under the wheels. Elijah hopped down with his oil can. The passengers stayed put. They waited. And waited some more.

"All aboard!" cried the conductor.

The pig was greased and ready to go.

Chug! Chug! Chug!

The passengers looked out at the passing farms. They talked. They ate. They laughed.

Half an hour later – *screeeeech!*

Time to grease the pig again.

What a job! Elijah didn't know which part he hated more – feeding the firebox or oiling the engine.

The train's metal parts needed oil to work smoothly. Without oil, the parts would stick and wear down. The train would stop.

While Elijah scooped coal, his mind sparked with ideas. Could he invent an oil cup that oiled the engine while the train was running? Every night after work, Elijah made drawings. Finally, he had a drawing of an oil cup he knew would work.

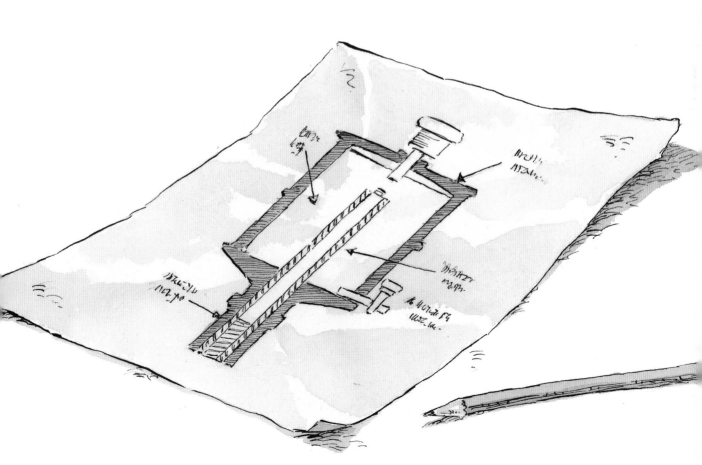

It took two years for Elijah to make a model of his oil cup. In 1872, he applied for a patent to protect his invention. Then he took the metal cup to work.

"There's a hole here to let the oil drip out," Elijah told the boss. "It drips oil when oil is needed. It drips it *where* it's needed. It's simple. Why not give it a try?"

Surprisingly, the boss agreed. Elijah attached the cup to the engine.

"Just for the Kalamazoo run," added the boss gruffly.

The train rumbled off, heading for Kalamazoo, Michigan. The engine huffed and puffed. Smoke billowed from its stack. The wheels clacked. The train chugged along for half an hour. *Chug! Chug! Chug!*

Everyone wondered when the train would stop. But it didn't. It chugged along for another half hour. And another.

Elijah McCoy's oil cup worked! It oiled the engine while the train was running. The train reached Kalamazoo in record time. The grease monkey was safe. Elijah was happy.

Elijah McCoy's oil cup made train travel faster and safer. Elijah worked on engine inventions all his life. He followed his dream. When Elijah got older, he encouraged children to stay in school and to follow their dreams too.

The Real McCoy!

Have you ever heard someone say they want the "real McCoy?" It means they want the real thing – no knockoffs, no substitutes. Other inventors copied Elijah McCoy's oil cup, but their drip cups didn't work as well. When engineers wanted to make sure they got the best oil cup, they asked for the real McCoy.

   Was Elijah McCoy a one-hit wonder? No way. He was an inventing marvel. During his lifetime, he filed 57 patents – more than any other Black inventor. Most of his inventions had to do with engines, but several did not. Elijah invented a portable ironing board, a lawn sprinkler, and even a better rubber heel for shoes. Want the best quality? Ask for the real McCoy!